THE PRINCIPLES
OF OUR WORLD ™

A collection of stories about how the
PRINCIPLE OF COURAGE
can help us along the journey of life

Written by
David Esposito

COURAGE

Independently published by Harvest Time Partners, Inc.
www.harvesttimepartners.com

Layout and illustrations by Imbue, The Marketing Agency at Digital Dog Direct.
www.imbuecreative.com

For additional information and permissions, please contact:
Harvest Time Partners, Inc.
Attention: David Anthony Esposito
Email: david@harvesttimepartners.com
Phone: 1-877-786-4278 or 269-370-9275

Harvest Time Partners, Inc.
ISBN-13: 978-0692246931 (Custom Universal)
ISBN-10: 0692246932

Dedicated to my Mom and Dad,
Mabel and Anthony Esposito.

Thank you for giving me the gift of a
strong foundation. It has meant more
than you will ever know.

About the Author

David Esposito is a combat veteran, business executive, husband, father, and creator of character-building resources that help individuals, families, and organizations reach their full potential.

He has developed award-winning resources under the brand Character Creates Opportunity®, a character-development initiative designed for all ages. He is also the inventor of Abundant Harvest® and Face to Face®: award-winning conversation games that are being utilized in families, schools, counseling programs, and faith-based organizations worldwide. The games help families and educators open the door to more effective communication and encourage decision making based on principles such as honesty, loyalty, and commitment with the intent of reinforcing the law of the harvest, simply, you "reap what you sow." Abundant Harvest and Face to Face help foster effective conversations on real-world issues and develop the critical life skill of face-to-face communication that is rapidly being replaced by today's online chatter.

David's character and leadership skills were cultivated at West Point and through leadership assignments in the US Army Infantry. As an airborne ranger infantry officer, David led a rifle platoon with the 101st Airborne Division through several combat operations in the Gulf War. He was recognized with a Bronze Star for combat operations in February 1991.

After launching his business career as a top sales representative, David quickly rose through the ranks of corporate America advancing to become the president of a $100-million-plus medical diagnostics company.

David and his wife Tracy founded and sponsor the Harvest Time Partners Foundation, a charitable organization that supports children and young adults in the pursuit of character-building opportunities worldwide. The Foundation supports a wide range of initiatives from college scholarships to community-service projects, as well as international efforts to reduce the suffering of children and young adults.

David provides support to individuals, families, and organizations on a variety of topics and subjects encompassing personal and executive development, team building, leadership training, and building a strong marriage and family. You can contact him at david@harvesttimepartners.com or by calling (877) 786-4278.

Visit www.harvesttimepartners.com to learn more.

What's Inside?

A Note to Parents and Teachers in the Home, the School, and the Community

There is no greater impact that we can make in this world than guiding children to develop the skills and abilities to most effectively handle life's ups and downs. Children are the builders of the future for our families and society, and we need to give them the best tools possible.

As much as we would like to "protect" children from the challenges of this world, the reality is that we cannot protect them forever. We would be wise to focus our efforts on preparation rather than protection in order to prepare them for the unavoidable reality that they will encounter challenges during their journey through life.

Aristotle wrote, "Good habits formed at youth make all the difference."

We have a responsibility as parents and teachers to help children form good habits and give them one of the greatest gifts: a strong foundation for living. A foundation that will support them in effectively dealing with the situations they will encounter in life.

There will always be new ideas and new techniques to support us in our changing world. However, even as techniques may change, we need consistent reminders that principles like honesty, loyalty, and commitment will remain the most effective foundation to form our decisions and actions, regardless of the changes in the world around us.

Our hope is that this book will be a helpful reminder to you and the children in your care about the importance of **The Principles** of honesty, teamwork, compassion, courage, and so many others.

The Principles can act as a compass to guide us through all the situations we encounter in life.

The Principles help individuals build and strengthen their character and *Character Creates Opportunity*® for a successful life, regardless of our situation.

There is a moment of time between our situation and how we respond.
In that moment of time, we have complete freedom to choose our response.
*The **inner voice** that drives our response is our **character**.*

The Principles arrive in that moment of time to help guide our response
based on a principle like honesty, compassion, and loyalty,
*which will build and strengthen our **character**.*

The Principles bring truth and lend strength to our inner voice.

As you use this book to help build a strong foundation in children, we hope it also serves
as a good reminder to you about the importance of living a life according to principles.

A Note to Children

Life is an exciting journey filled with fun, excitement, wonder, and, sometimes, struggles and challenges.

Have you ever ridden a roller coaster?

Life is like riding a roller coaster.

There is so much excitement in the beginning as you get ready to jump in the seat and start the ride. We all must buckle up for safety as the roller coaster will have many ups and downs, twists and turns; so buckling up is the smart thing to do.

There will be times when you will be so high on the roller coaster that you can see everything that is all around you. You will see the exciting turns ahead, and you will know exactly what is coming next.

Then, all of a sudden, you will be in a dark tunnel and a little bit scared because you cannot see what is in front of you.

Then, you speed out of the tunnel into the light again. You're back to enjoying the twists and turns and ups and downs once again.

Life is like a roller coaster ride. This book was written to help prepare you for the "roller coaster" of life.

In this book, you will learn about **The Principles**.

The Principles will help keep you safe during the ups and downs and twists and turns of life, just like the seat belt on the roller coaster.

The Principles will always be at your side to help you during the greatest roller coaster ride—your LIFE!

Now, get ready to buckle up with **The Principles.** Have fun!

The Principle of Courage

"Hello, I am The Principle of Courage.

"People say that I am the reminder they need to be brave when they feel worried and afraid.

"There will be times in your life when you are afraid. We all get afraid.

"I will help you to be brave and strong when you are afraid.

"You are stronger than your fears, and I will help remind you of your strength.

"My parents told me that even though I am small, I have the strength to face giants and overcome my fears. That is why they named me Courage.

"Please call on me when you need help to face your fears. I can help remind you of your strength.

"I will be there to support and encourage you—no matter what situations you experience in life.

"Please, count on me to help you be courageous."

Courage in Our Home

Jimmy spent a great deal of time driving with his older brother Joey. Their parents both worked long hours, and Jimmy needed Joey to drive him to all his activities like soccer practice and guitar lessons.

Joey sometimes looked at his smartphone while he was driving. Joey would send text messages as well. Jimmy knew that it was not safe to text and drive. Their parents told Joey many times that he should not text while he was driving.

One day, Jimmy spoke up to his older brother and said, "Joey, please don't text and drive because we might get into an accident. It is not safe."

Joey said, "Jimmy, don't tell me what to do! I know what I am doing; and I am a safe driver. If you want a ride to your practice each day, then just be quiet and let me drive the way I want to drive."

Jimmy was afraid to stand up to his older brother Joey because he was very big and strong. Also, Jimmy really needed a ride to his practices each day.

In a moment of time, a number of thoughts raced through Jimmy's mind.

Jimmy thought, "I am really scared about getting into a car accident when Joey texts while he drives. He knows it is wrong, but he keeps doing it. Every time I tell him to stop, he always yells back at me and threatens not to drive me to practice each day. I really don't want to miss practice."

"Everyone gets a little scared when their older brother yells at them," said The Principle of Courage. "I know you are worried that Joey will not drive you to practice if you keep telling him to stop texting. It is really scary to be riding in a car when someone is texting and driving.

"However, as The Principle of Courage, I want to tell you that you know your brother is doing something wrong that could result in someone getting hurt. Texting and driving is wrong and very unsafe. In addition, your parents have told Joey not to text and drive.

"The right thing to do is to be strong and stand up to Joey until he stops texting and driving."

In that moment of time, Jimmy thought about what The Principle of Courage said about being strong to face his fears; and he decided what to do.

"Joey!" Jimmy spoke with courage and strength. "It is not safe to text and drive! We could get into an accident and hurt others and ourselves. I am not going to drive in the car anymore, and I would rather walk to practice than ride with you. I know mom and dad will not be happy about why I have started to walk to practice. Please stop!"

Jimmy looked directly into his older brother's eyes when he spoke to him.

Joey could tell Jimmy was serious. This was the first time that Jimmy really stood up to him and did not back down.

Joey thought about it for a moment and said, "Okay, Jimmy. You are right. I should not text and drive. It is not safe. I am sorry, and I will not do it again. Thanks for reminding me about how foolish I am when I text and drive."

The Principle of Courage helped remind Jimmy about being strong to overcome his fears.

Later that evening, as Jimmy lay in bed ready to go to sleep, The Principle of Courage came to his bedside.

The Principle of Courage said, "Jimmy, I am really glad that you chose to be strong today and overcome your fears.

"I know you were scared, but you demonstrated courage by standing up to your older brother Joey about texting and driving.

"Please remember to be strong to overcome your fears when you encounter similar situations in life."

Courage in Our School

The middle school bus stop was always crowded in the morning as kids waited for the bus to arrive. Mary normally stood quietly as her sixth-grade classmates talked about all sorts of things.

Mary overheard some of the girls talking about the new outfits they were wearing. They all seemed so excited about wearing their new clothes. The girls looked over at Hannah, who was standing next to Mary, and said with a smirk, "Hey, Hannah, it looks like you are wearing the same old ripped-up clothes that you always wear. I guess you like wearing old messy clothes."

Mary could tell that those words hurt Hannah, but she was not saying anything in response to the mean girls. Mary felt bad because she knew Hannah's family did not have a lot of money for new clothes, and she was probably too hurt to defend herself.

In a moment of time, a number of thoughts raced through Mary's mind.

Mary thought, "Those girls are so mean to Hannah. They have no idea that her family does not have the money for new clothes. I feel really bad for her. However, I am afraid those girls will say mean things to me if I jump into the conversation. Maybe I should just stay quiet and act like I did not hear anything."

What should I do?

In that moment of time, The Principle of Courage came to Mary's side.

Hi, Mary. It looks like you might need my help.

"We all get a little scared and confused when we are in these kinds of situations," said The Principle of Courage. "I know you can tell that Hannah is sad about the comments those girls are making about her clothes. Also, it is normal to worry about what might happen when we start getting involved in other people's problems.

"However, as The Principle of Courage, I want to tell you that you know it is not right for those girls to tease Hannah. They are being mean to her about her clothes. Also, Hannah is a quiet girl and never seems to be able to defend herself.

"The right thing to do is to be strong and brave to help defend Hannah."

In that moment of time, Mary thought about what The Principle of Courage said about being strong to face her fears; and she decided what to do.

"Hey, girls!" Mary spoke up with courage and strength. "It is not right to make fun of Hannah and her clothes. You should just be thankful that you have nice clothes. Stop saying mean things to other people whose parents can't buy them the things that your parents buy for you."

Mary looked directly into the eyes of the girls who were being mean to Hannah.

The girls were shocked that Mary spoke up because she was normally very quiet at the bus stop. They knew she was serious and that she was right. One of the girls said to Mary, "You are right. We are not being nice to Hannah when we tease her about her clothes."

All three girls turned to Hannah and said, "We are sorry."

The Principle of Courage helped remind Mary about overcoming fear and being strong to stand up for what is right.

Later that evening, as Mary lay in bed ready to go to sleep, The Principle of Courage came to her bedside.

The Principle of Courage said, "Mary, I am really glad that you chose to be strong today and overcome your fears.

"I know you were scared, but you demonstrated courage by standing up to those girls who were making fun of Hannah and the clothes she was wearing.

"Please remember to be strong to overcome your fears when you encounter similar situations in life."

Mary, you can sleep well tonight because you did the right thing today.

Courage in Our Parents

Jill and her brother Stephen were sitting down to dinner with their mother. "Where is Dad?" asked Jill.

"He is finishing up a big project at work and will be home soon," answered Jill's mom Carol.

Just as their mom finished speaking, their father came rushing into the kitchen and said, "I am home! Just in time for dinner!"

"Yeah!" said the kids as they all sat down to eat.

"That was cutting it close, Bill," said Carol with a frustrated tone of voice.

As they all began to enjoy dinner, the kids could tell that there was a little tension between their mom and dad.

"Bill," said Carol. "I am really tired of you working late and getting home just in time to eat. We hardly have any time to sit together as a family. And when you do come home, you have your smartphone sitting right in front of you waiting for another message from work."

Jill and Stephen could hear their mother's voice getting louder and louder.

"This is a really busy time at work," said Bill. "It will get better soon; and, besides, even when I do come home, you also have your smartphone out and barely pick up your head to have a conversation."

Jill and Stephen could tell this was the start of another argument between their parents.

Carol was really starting to get upset.

In a moment of time, a number of thoughts raced through Carol's mind.

Carol thought to herself, "Jim is really being mean. I work all day and hurry home to get dinner ready with the kids while he takes his time coming home. I only glance at my phone to catch up with a few friends that I have not talked to all day because I have been busy at work. However, I know he is really stressed out with this big project at work. I know it is not easy for him right now."

Hi, Carol. It looks like you might need my help.

In that moment of time, The Principle of Courage came to Carol's side.

What should I do?

"Sometimes, we all can get a little upset when we are very busy with work and family," said The Principle of Courage. "I know you are working hard and look forward to some time to relax with your family and friends in the evening. In addition, Bill is very stressed out about this big project at work. Also, I know you both do not like to have these kinds of arguments at the dinner table with the kids.

"However, as The Principle of Courage, I want to tell you that during tough times like this, it is important to be strong and brave to find a better way to handle these situations. Yelling at each other is not going to solve the problem. It never has before, so why do you think it will this time?

"The right thing to do is to be strong and brave to ask Bill to help find a better way."

In that moment of time, Carol thought about what The Principle of Courage said about being strong and brave to find a better way in facing these challenges with Bill.

"Bill, I know we both don't want to keep arguing like this anymore. What do you say we try a better way?"

"Sure," said Bill. "What do you have in mind?"

"I know we are both busy coming home from work and just need some time to rest after our long days," said Carol. "How about at dinner we put away our smartphones and focus on family time. We can always go back to our smartphones after we put the kids to bed."

"Carol, that makes a lot of sense. That really is a better way. Let's do it!" said Bill.

The Principle of Courage helped remind Carol to be strong and brave to look for a better way to help her family.

Later that evening, as Carol lay in bed ready to go to sleep, The Principle of Courage came to her bedside.

The Principle of Courage said, "Carol, I am really glad that you chose to be strong today and look for a better way to address the problems with your family.

"I know you were angry and frustrated, but you demonstrated courage by reaching out to Bill to try to find a better way to handle your busy family life.

"Please remember to be strong and look for a better way when you encounter similar situations in life."

Courage in Our Work

Paul's father Mark works as a teller in a bank. He helps people deposit their money in the bank and encourages them to save their money. Paul's father does the same thing at home when he encourages Paul to save his money in a piggy bank he keeps in his bedroom.

Mark was working late on a Friday when a large number of people came in to deposit their paychecks.

Mark began to get nervous when he saw so many people lining up. He could hear the customers complaining about how long it was taking to deposit their money. In order for Mark to get people through the line quickly, he needed to ask his manager for some help. However, Mark was a little afraid about what his manager might think of him, if he asked for help.

In a moment of time, a number of thoughts raced through Mark's mind.

Mark thought to himself, "Wow, there is no way I can get all these people through the line quickly. I really need some help. However, if I ask my manager for help, he might think that I am not smart enough to do this job. He may replace me with someone else who can do the job better."

What should I do?

In that moment of time, The Principle of Courage came to Mark's side.

Hi, Mark. It looks like you might need my help.

"We all get nervous from time to time at work," said The Principle of Courage. "When there is a long line of customers that need our help, it is very easy to get worried about what to do. I know it is also difficult to ask your manager for help. You want your manager to know that you can do the job on your own.

"However, as The Principle of Courage, I want to tell you that during times like this at work, it is important to be strong and ask for help. Asking for help is not a sign of weakness; it is sign of strength to be comfortable asking others for help to do a great job. The customers need to be helped as fast as possible, and you cannot do it alone. Your manager is there to help you. The right thing to do is to be strong and brave to ask your manager for help to move the customers through the line quickly."

Mark, I will be right by your side as you decide what to do.

In that moment of time, Mark thought about what The Principle of Courage said about being strong and asking for help.

Mark picked up the office phone and called his manager: "I need some help up at the bank deposit line. There are a lot of customers, and I could use some help to get them through the line quickly. Thank you."

Mark's manager came out of his office right away to help the rest of the customers make their deposits. With Mark and his manager working together, they were able to get all the customers through the line quickly.

The Principle of Courage helped remind Mark to be strong and ask for help when he needed it.

Later that evening, as Mark lay in bed ready to go to sleep, The Principle of Courage came to his bedside.

The Principle of Courage said, "Mark, I am really glad that you chose to be strong today and ask your manager for help.

"I know you were afraid of what your manager might think of you, but you demonstrated courage by asking for help and working together to move the customers through the line quickly.

"Please remember to be strong and courageous when you encounter similar situations in life."

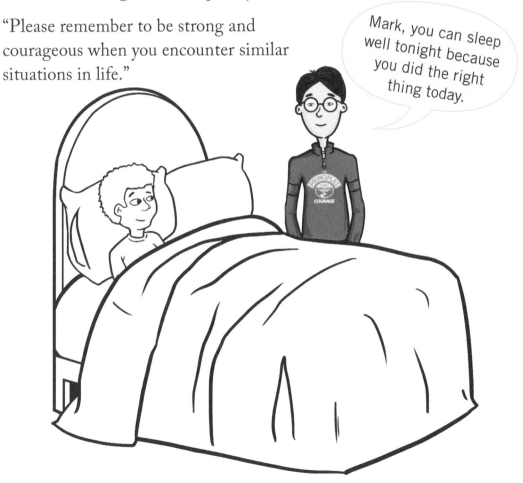

Mark, you can sleep well tonight because you did the right thing today.

Where Do We Go from Here?

"Hello, again. It is me, The Principle of Courage.

"I hope you enjoyed reading about the different situations in life, and how I can help you to be brave and strong when you are fearful of some pretty difficult situations.

"I want to encourage you to keep working on facing your fears every day of your life. Just like practicing your favorite sport or playing your favorite instrument, practicing to be brave and strong every day will help you grow stronger in your ability to be courageous.

"As you get older, the situations in life will get harder; and you will need to be strong to make sure you can still act with courage when life gets more difficult.

"On the next page of this book, there are some situations where you can practice being brave and strong to help prepare you for the times you encounter these situations in your life.

"Please call on me when you need help to face your fears. I can help remind you of your strength.

"I will be there to support and encourage you—no matter what situations you experience in life.

"Please, count on me to help you be courageous."

What Would YOU Do?

We will all experience some situations in life when we should choose to remember The Principle of Courage.

Below are some sample situations to think about how you would respond.

Remember **The Principle of Courage**

"What would YOU do?"

Each person in the class has to give a speech today. Your teacher asks, "Who wants to go first?" What would YOU do?	You have a substitute teacher for math class. The "class clown" continues to cause trouble for the young teacher, and it is becoming very distracting to the class. What would YOU do?
When you are shopping in a local sports store, you notice someone putting a pair of new sneakers in their backpack and heading out the door. What would YOU do?	You are working hard in a summer job at a fast food restaurant. As you are making some hamburgers, you look up and notice one of your co-workers taking some money from the cash register and putting it in his pocket. What would YOU do?
A big bully at school is really starting to pick on you. You are afraid and anxious about going to school. What would YOU do?	While on the playground at recess you notice some kids making fun of someone because he does not have the "trendy, new clothes" that many of the other kids wear. His family does not have a lot of money, and he is usually wearing clothes that used to be worn by his older brothers. What would YOU do?

Some Additional Resources to Help
Award-Winning Conversation Games

As our world has become more connected with things like the internet, smart phones, and social media, today's online chatter has actually caused our families to become more disconnected; and we are losing the critical life-skill of effective face to face communication.

Harvest Time Partners created a series of conversation games called Abundant Harvest® and Face to Face® to help families and educators open the door to more effective communication and encourage decision making based on principles such as honesty and loyalty with the intent of reinforcing the Law of the Harvest, simply, "you reap what you sow." Abundant Harvest and Face to Face conversation games provide parents and teachers with teachable moments and quality time with their children.

Spend quality time discussing real-world situations with your children and students!

Having a difficult time getting teenagers to "open-up" about dealing with their reality? Abundant Harvest for Teens & Adults can help!

Start great conversations with Face to Face, a fast paced, travel ready conversation game!

Kids Edition

For ages 7 and up

Teen Edition

For teenagers 13 and up

Dinner Party Edition

For ages 18 and up, adults and parents

Visit www.harvesttimepartners.com to learn more!

Some Additional Resources to Help
The Principles of Our World Children's Books

The Principle of Honesty	The Principle of Teamwork	The Principle of Sacrifice	The Principle of Courage	The Principle of Compassion
"People say that I am the reminder they need to remain truthful in all that they say and do."	"People say that I am the reminder they need to work together to accomplish great things."	"People say that I am the reminder they need to think about others instead of themselves."	"People say that I am the reminder they need to be brave when they feel worried and afraid."	"People say that I am the reminder they need to reach out to help people in need."

    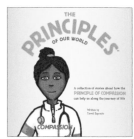

Visit www.harvesttimepartners.com to learn more!

CPSIA information can be obtained at www.ICGtesting.com
Printed in the USA
LVOW01s2352071114

412606LV00003B/13/P

9 780692 246931